PERCEPTION

THE ART OF RIGHT SEEING

PASTOR KAREEM JACKSON

INTRODUCTION

P erception is the process of becoming aware and how we respond to external realities, hardships, and the unknown mysteries of life. When you were first born, you were given a perception that was shaped by your parents of how things should be accomplished in turbulent times, how your character should be carried, and even how your lifestyle should look. Yet as you got older, you started to see that many things you were taught as a child started to become tainted by your environment, by your relationships, and by your experiences. Your perception of life was through lenses that weren't so clear anymore. They began to carry the stains of hurt, shame, regret, fears, and an identity imbalance. Sometimes what we fail to realize is that these stains have the power to spill over into our behaviors, our mindset, our drive and even our relationship with God. Before we know it, we find ourselves getting further and further from who we were created to be. It catapulted us into thinking that we are in a deep, dark hole with no one there to rescue us due to our stained perception. We were once this person full of life, ready to conquer any hardship life threw at us and go full force upon accomplishing the purpose that is on your lives. Yet, now as we look in the mirror after we endured failures, delays, and silence from God, we respond to life in defeat.

Wondering when will it be our turn, when will this pain end, and how long will this last? Your let downs have driven you into a decision to just give up until God sends you a light through your dark seasons. He extends to you a promise that once you connect to Him, you will take on His perfected vision, His infinite wisdom, His sound mind, His perception, and kingdom mysteries. God has the power to take your stained lenses and cleanse them in His blood and transcend you into the person that He created you to become. It all begins with you choosing whether to break all that you once knew and allowing God to birth in you a new mindset, a new perception, and to shape everything attached to you into His image and likeness. The road from trial to triumph awaits you, this is the Art of Right Seeing.

TABLE OF CONTENTS

CHAPTER 1

THE RIGHT PERCEPTION OF DISCIPLESHIP

Mark 8:34-38 (NASB)

[34] *And He summoned the crowd with His disciples, and said to them, "If anyone wishes to come after Me, he must deny himself, and take up his cross and follow Me.*

[35] *"For whoever wishes to save his life will lose it, but whoever loses his life for My sake and the gospel will save it.*

[36] *"For what does it profit a man to gain the whole world, and forfeit his soul?*

[37] *"For what will a man give in exchange for his soul?*

[38] *"For whoever is ashamed of Me and My words in this adulterous and sinful generation, the Son of Man will also be ashamed of him when He comes in the glory of His Father with the holy angels."*

Perception is the sensory experience of the world. Our perception connects us to the world that's around us all. One of the greatest issues that we have is not really what we see but how we see what we see. Many of our misconceptions about Jesus as we read in the scriptures is the seeing issue. What I mean by seeing issues is that since perception connects us to our world, if we can't see right then, the understanding is hindered. We can read the scripture and know the letter of what we read and yet miss the revelation of what Jesus is trying to release to us. In the context of these verses, I wanted to convey the issue of perception and show us that the problem with the disciples, as well as a lot of us as believers, is that we have a problem with our perception. It's the seeing issue. If we don't see right, then the things that we do see will be interpreted wrong. I also wanted to convey that the Lord uses the eye's perception to get to the training of the mind. The missing truth is that our mentality has to be disciplined for us to be all that God wants us to be. If the mind isn't trained, then the behavior won't adequately change. There will be a mental blockage that hinders true discipleship. What Jesus was doing with the disciples was trying to show them that being a disciple is not about all of the ups that can come with us being a disciple, but in our walk, with the Lord, there will be some necessary obstacles that we must endure. The reason that it's necessary is that it's a part of the training of the eyes. Jesus tells them that he has to go to Jerusalem and must suffer many things and be rejected by the elders and chief priests and scribes and be killed and after three days rise again. The problem with the disciples is because they couldn't see Jesus right then, they couldn't understand the totality of his assignment, and as a result, the cross became a stumbling block for Israel. They wanted a Messiah that would establish a kingdom to overthrow Rome. They didn't see that Jesus was going to have to suffer, die, and rise again to set up the kingdom that he had been referring to. His kingdom was not of the earth realm, meaning that the way to establish it couldn't be normal. In John 18:36, Jesus says," My kingdom is not of this world. If it were, my servants would fight to prevent my arrest by the Jewish leaders. But now my kingdom is from another place. Since the disciples didn't see Jesus right, they misunderstood the methodology that he used to establish his kingdom.

Peter takes Jesus aside and rebukes him and Jesus seeing the disciples, Jesus turns and rebukes Peter and says," Get behind me Satan, because your mind is on man's interests, not God's." He is rebuking Peter because Peter let Satan invade his mind, and it came out in his language. It's critical to emphasize here that we must be careful not to let the enemy gain access to your mind. What it does is, it comes out of your mouth, and it will affect your relationship with God. Peter is upset because he got the revelation of who Jesus was, and now Jesus makes an announcement that he is about to leave. It's mind-boggling, but it again reiterates the issue of perception. It's hard to grasp that Jesus would give them insight into the fact that he is the Messiah, the Son of God, and then in the same breath tell them that I am leaving. The problem was, they perceived that Jesus had come to stay. They couldn't see that Jesus came to leave. They were downcast because of a mental blockage due to faulty perception. Perception is everything. We have to be sure that what we see has a chance to be processed in our minds. Then we let the spirit of God give clarity so that you can have the right perception of what God is trying to show you. God has got to give understanding to what we see. See, the problem was more than theological; it was very practical. Jesus had called these men to follow Him, and they knew that whatever happened to Him would happen to them. If there were a cross in His future, then since we are connected to him, there would be one in their future as well. For them, they didn't get with Jesus to die. They got with him to live. Here is where the wrong perception shows up. In the kingdom, things seem to be the opposite. The way up is down. The way to exaltation is humiliation. The way to get notoriety is to be a servant. The necessary obstacles for the disciples are that you have to deal with some issues if you're going to be connected to Jesus. Despite their devotion to Him, the disciples were still ignorant of the true relationship between the cross and the crown. They were following Satan's philosophy (glory without suffering) instead of God's philosophy (suffering transformed into glory). The perception that you hold will determine the philosophy you prescribe too. The philosophy you accept will determine how you live and how you serve. We see this in the church today. When people don't perceive our relationship with God right, then we see that the mentality is that we aren't supposed to go through anything. Everything is supposed to be a bed of roses, and life is only supposed to give us what causes us to prosper. Those who hold the wrong perception see suffering as an anomaly that has nothing to do with the believer, but that is poor perception. It's Satan's philosophy that suggests that if you're suffering, then you must not be in the will of God. Those who have the right seeing vantage of our relationship with God can understand that it's through the suffering that we achieve glory. Paul tells Timothy in 2 Timothy 2:12 if we suffer, we shall also reign with him; if we deny him, he also will deny us. The word suffer in that passage is translated as endure.

4

It's the Greek word hypoménō. It means to remain and stay under. It means to bear the trials. When you and I understand seeing our relationship with God right, then we know that the things we endure will pay off for us if we can bear it. If we have endured what we are facing, then God will get the glory, and we will, in turn, get the blessing. I want to encourage somebody that will read this and might be facing the worst season of your life. If you can endure it with the right perception, God will work things out in your favor. We have to make sure that we perceive correctly that everything has a cost. That includes following Jesus.

Here is the right perception of being a disciple of Jesus Christ. Discipleship has a high price tag. There are a few things that this Mark 8 passage suggests. First, we have to surrender ourselves. We all have this issue of self-indulgence vs. self-denial. We have choices to make. Jesus says that any person who wishes (*thelei*): to desire, wish, design, purpose, resolve, determine. It is a deliberate will, a deliberate choice, a determined resolve to follow Christ. If a person really wishes and deliberately chooses to follow Christ, then he has to deny self. It must be understood that this is not something that God will make you do. It has to be voluntary. God, in His love, will not force us to make this decision. It is the individual who wills and chooses; therefore, it is the individual who must act and do denying of self. That reveals to us that if we make the choice, then it becomes our responsibility to commit the surrender.

Deny (*aparneomai*): to disown, disregard, forsake, renounce, reject, refuse, restrain, disclaim, do without. It means to subdue, to disregard oneself and one's interest. Very simply put, it means to say "no." The call is not to say "no" to some behavior or thing, but to say no to *self*. A person is to *deny self*. This means much more than just being negative, that is, giving up something and doing without something. It means that we are to act positively, to say "yes" to Christ and "no" to self. It means to let Christ rule and reign in one's heart and life, to let Christ have His way completely in us. Of course, if a person allows Christ to rule in his life, all negative, as well as positive behavior, is taken care of. That's where the perception comes in again because you have to see that you are not the one that is in charge when you come after Christ. Oftentimes we have a problem with the word of God because, for the believer, it's the governing authority for our lives. We have the proclivity to believe that the word of God is too restrictive. That it hinders our ability to live our best lives. That is because we have the wrong perception of the word of God. Those so-called restrictions are really protective measures designed to help you deny the desires of the flesh. The flesh always desires to have its indulgences gratified. It's through the willful surrender to the instructions of the Lord that we can suffocate the desires and impulses of the flesh.

Follow (*akoloutheō*): to be a follower or companion, to be a disciple. It has the idea of seeking to be in union with and in the likeness of. It is following Christ, seeking to be just like Him. Again, this is not passive behavior but an active commitment and walk. It is energy and effort, action, and work. It is going after Christ with zeal and energy, struggling and seeking to follow in His footsteps no matter the cost. It's Christlike to the highest degree. It's what Paul addresses in Romans 8:29 For those he foreknew he also predestined to be conformed to the image of his Son, that he might be the firstborn among many brothers and sisters. Conformed in this context in Romans is the Greek word symmorphos, meaning fashioned like unto or jointly formed. It means to be like. Meaning in order to follow Christ, we have to be willing to be formed and fashioned in his likeness. Whatever you follow will form you. Paul brings this thought into plain view when he writes in 1 Corinthians 15:33 Don't be deceived: evil communications corrupt good manners. If you surround yourself with evil speaking, thinking, and perceptions, then it will form you. That's why it's crucial for us to understand that we have to be careful what and who we follow.

Secondly, we must identify with Christ in his suffering and death. Here we must address the issue of saving our life versus losing our life. Jesus declares that if a man wishes to save his life, then he has to lose it. Each of us that are believers has to abandon his life. Desires and goals and even perceptions that are connected to the world and has to sacrifice all that he/she is and has for the cause of Christ. The person who is willing to surrender at this level will actually save his life. On the counter, the person who keeps his life and what he has makes it his life mission to seek more and more of what he has will, in turn, lose his life completely and eternally. When a person is seeking to save his own life, that is the individual who wants to avoid aging. They want to avoid decaying. That person wants to make their life more comfortable and secure at the expense of neglecting a relationship with Jesus Christ. They want to gain wealth and power but compromise their relationship with God. Those people will lose their life. Whosoever shall lose his life for the gospel, the same shall save it." That says that I have to have the right perception of the importance of the gospel. The gospel doesn't promote a suffering-free life. It actually shows us the suffering way is the Jesus way. I grow from what I overcome. Real growth comes from the ability to empty myself of trying to control the outcome of my own life and let God grow me up.

Finally, we have to follow Christ obediently. Discipleship is a matter of profit and loss, a question of whether we will *waste* our lives or *invest* our lives. Jesus gives a warning that we need to address, and that is once we have spent our lives, we can't buy it back. What Jesus is showing the disciples, as well as every believer here and now, you have to see the life of discipleship right to get the best out of it. You have one life to live, and after that, you're done. The message is plain and simple. Make this life count. You might gain the whole world but lose your soul. It's the equivalent of a wasted life. You might be a success in the eyes of men and yet have nothing to show for your life when you stand before God. Be careful, child of God, what you perceive to be success. It's not about what you accumulated on the earth, but what you did with your life while you were here. If your perception is right, then you know the truth of gaining the world, and that is, THERE IS NO SUCH THING AS GAINING THE WHOLE WORLD! Right perception reveals everything in the earth realm is temporary, but the soul is eternal. The soul is more important than anything that is fading. The reward for following this level of obedience is becoming just like Jesus and sharing in his glory. Satan promises you glory, but in the end, you receive suffering. God promises you suffering, but in the end, that suffering is transformed into glory. If we acknowledge Christ and live for Him, He will one day acknowledge us and share His glory with us.

CHAPTER 2

UNLOCKING KINGDOM MYSTERIES

Matthew 13:10-17 (NASB)

[10] *And the disciples came and said to Him, "Why do You speak to them in parables?"*

[11] *Jesus answered them, "To you, it has been granted to know the mysteries of the kingdom of heaven, but to them, it has not been granted.*

[12] *"For whoever has, to him more shall be given, and he will have an abundance; but whoever does not have, even what he has shall be taken away from him.*

[13] *"Therefore I speak to them in parables; because while seeing they do not see, and while hearing they do not hear, nor do they understand.*

[14] *"In their case, the prophecy of Isaiah is being fulfilled, which says, 'YOU WILL KEEP ON HEARING, BUT WILL NOT UNDERSTAND; YOU WILL KEEP ON SEEING BUT WILL NOT PERCEIVE.*

15 FOR THE HEART OF THIS PEOPLE HAS BECOME DULL, WITH THEIR EARS THEY SCARCELY HEAR, AND THEY HAVE CLOSED THEIR EYES. OTHERWISE, THEY WOULD SEE WITH THEIR EYES, HEAR WITH THEIR EARS, AND UNDERSTAND WITH THEIR HEART AND RETURN, AND I WOULD HEAL THEM.'

16 "But blessed are your eyes because they see; and your ears, because they hear.

17 "For truly I say to you that many prophets and righteous men desired to see what you see, and did not see it, and to hear what you hear, and did not hear it.

God is a God of relationship. Everything about God speaks of relationship, closeness, unity, and fellowship with him. If we were to probe that thought a little deeper, we could see that the reason Jesus came to die for our sins is that the sin of Adam disconnected us. Jesus came to reconnect us because we were made to have relationships with God. In his holiness, God cannot have a relationship to sin, so he set up a way for man to have fellowship with him through the sacrifice of his only begotten Son. This sacrifice was once and for all. Relationships are designed for the purpose of trust and openness with intentionality. That says that every person that we meet is a potential relationship. We, as human beings, are socially programmed. We work hard to find and build good relationships with other people. We affiliate and attract different people at different stages of our life.

Whether you are spiritual or unspiritual, in church or the corporate community, we have to invest the time to gain a greater relationship because there are benefits that are connected to those relationships. When it comes to God, there are things that God will only show to people that are intimately connected to him. When Jesus came on the scene, he came proclaiming the mysteries of the kingdom. Mystery is the Greek word mustérion, a mystery, secret, of which initiation is necessary; in the New Testament, it deals with the counsels of God, once hidden but now revealed in the Gospel. A mystery can be known, but it is only known to those who are in the realm of revelation and connected to the revelator. In the case of the believer, the only person who gives revelation is God. Jesus came to reveal God to mankind. Jesus revealed the eternal plan of the Father that he had proposed since the foundation of the world. The key to understand is that you and I have a big part in the plan of God. The only way for us to know the role we play is to have those mysteries unlocked to us. That suggests that everything that we can or will receive from God hinges on us knowing Him. We have to know his truth and then walk those truths out in obedience. Jesus is saying that if you have knowledge of the mysteries of the kingdom, then he will release more in abundance. As we advance in the kingdom the more, then we grab hold of keys that will unlock blessings and victory for us.

These verses in this chapter reveal a day of crisis in Jesus' ministry. The religious leaders are now growing in opposition to Jesus, and Jesus is aware of these things. Jesus then explains to his disciples that he will be opposed by the religious leaders and then his crucifixion and resurrection. Their question to Jesus is what will happen to this kingdom that you have been preaching about? The way Jesus answered their question is by a series of parables. Parables come from the Greek word parabole; a teaching aid cast alongside the truth being taught. The revelation to truth was housed in the parable. Jesus tells a parable about a sower and the seed. What he is trying to convey to the disciples is, "Your mind is a garden. Your thoughts are the seeds. You can grow flowers, or you can grow weeds." People working in the realm of technology have an idiom that says, "Garbage in garbage out." It means a bad input will result in bad output. If your premise is flawed, so too will your solution be flawed.

Simply put, this means if you cultivate poor or incorrect data—the seeds—you wind up perpetuating these messages both within yourself and among others. That's a whole field of weeds! It means being mindful, mindful of the quality of what you take in as well as what you produce. Mindful that you have a choice to choose positive values and direction. Mindful that what you plant inside will grow outside. Our mind takes in information, and then it comes out of us. I am floored oftentimes how we misunderstand the power of the environment in which we are planted. We are a sum total of the environment that we were subjected to. How we grew up and the people who taught us how to think, speak, live, and observe the world were all seeds that were implanted in our minds. One of those things took root in us then determined how we live. Some of us need to be reprogrammed from faulty seeds that were planted in us that have caused us to be cynical and pessimistic. We have to realize that the mind is hungry, so we have to be aware of what kind of diet we feed it. Be mindful not to let people plant garbage seeds in your mind because you will become a sum total of your thought life. You are what you think.

When people say, "Let me plant this thought in your mind," we express the idea of this parable. The seed is God's Word; the various soils represent different kinds of hearts, and the varied results show the different responses to the Word of God. It was not the first time that Jesus used parables, but the first time that he had spoken so many and some of such length. The text says that Jesus got out of the house and was by the sea, and large crowds gathered to see him. The next thing it said was that he spoke in parables to them. Jesus reveals that he isn't moved by crowds. Jesus sees the crowd but the purpose for the parable was the fact that you have people in the crowd that aren't interested in what he is really saying. In chapter 12, we see the rejection of the leaders of Israel when they say that Jesus is casting out demons by the power of Satan. You could imagine that some people were in the crowd that were spectators and unbelievers, so what Jesus did was change his method of communication to a method that would weed out those who connected to him and those who are just hanging around. I need to pause and tell you that we can't be moved by crowds because that doesn't dictate the blessing of God. There are all kinds of people that are in crowds. The issue with the crowd and perception is that we can all be in the same place, looking at the same thing, and even hearing the same words being planted in our minds, but depending on our spectrum of revelation, we won't get the same thing out of it. Have you ever been in a meeting with people, and you know that you all heard the same information, but it seems that some left with a different conclusion? Have you ever been in church with others and heard the sermon with other believers but hearing the conversation from many church members after the service, you gathered that everyone didn't come away with the same conclusion? The issue is perception. Jesus understands this, so he tells this parable.

It's critical that we know not only is Jesus not moved by crowds but also you have to have a disciplined mindset in order to understand the mysteries of the kingdom. In the first of seven parables in this chapter, Jesus talked about a farmer who sowed seed in his field. The emphasis in the story is on the results of the sowing, for the seed fell on four kinds of soil: along the path, on rocky places, among thorns, and on good soil. So, the farmer had four distinct kinds of results. The disciples noticed that Jesus had changed his communication approach, and now they want to inquire why. Jesus says to them, first, the revelation of this truth that is hidden is only for you who are connected to the kingdom mindset. To know the mysteries (gnōnai ta mustēria). In Greek grammar, this word is in the second aorist active infinitive of ginōskō. The word mustērion is from mustēs, one initiated, and that from mueō, to close or shut. The mystery-religions of the east had all sorts of secrets and signs as secret societies do today. But those initiated knew them. So, the disciples have been initiated into the secrets of the kingdom of heaven. Meaning that everyone isn't privy to the information that is connected to this secret way. That's why we need God to discipline our mindset to fix our perception of the kingdom because, without this eye-mind transformation, you will miss spiritual information. Remember that the crowd is around for the same parable. They all heard the same thing. They saw the same Jesus, but because of the level of connection, the disciples got information that others couldn't grasp. You and other people can see the same thing. The same situation, circumstances, the same problem, but depending on your perception, you can see God moving in it in a way that the crowd around you can't see because of where they sit in the area of perception. People trying to figure out how you praise God, dancing and shouting when things are bad around you? They don't know that you have a kingdom mindset, so what looks like a disaster to others is development for you. You know God is about to bust a move in your situation. You can be in a crowd that is in chaos, but you are sensitive in the spirit, so you can hear God telling you it's already alright while others are going crazy! They don't understand that you are in a different kingdom with a different eye vantage and a completely different mindset! You know that you don't have to wait until the battle is over! YOU CAN SHOUT NOW! Jesus says since the Jewish leaders have decided how they are going to perceive me, then I'll give my mysteries to those that want me! I think here we need to resolve that it's a privilege to be in the loop when it comes to kingdom mysteries. Then Kingdom truth was hidden from unbelievers. Isaiah wrote during a time of sweeping judgment on Judah. He had just pronounced a series of curses on the people for their drunkenness, debauchery, immorality, dishonesty, injustice, and hypocrisy. While Isaiah was preaching his message of doom, King Uzziah died, and the nation was plunged into some of its darkest days. They were on the verge of captivity by Babylon as part of God's judgment, yet they refused to turn to God for mercy and help. The people kept on hearing, but they did not understand, and they kept on seeing, but they did not perceive, because they had intentionally closed their eyes and their ears to God and refused to understand with their heart and return to Him for Him to heal them. Because they chose to ignore God and His word, God judicially locked them up in their unbelief so that they would fear His judgment.

The last thing this text teaches in the area of perception is that you need the right soil to understand the mysteries. Jesus tells his disciples that they have blessed eyes because they see and blessed ears because they hear. Remember that the issue in the parable isn't the sower because they all heard the word, but they had to have the right soil to receive what was spoken. Meaning that when a man or woman believes the word of God and he brings them into the kingdom, and then he downloads the truth to them as they walk with him. The believer can understand because the Holy Spirit is in them, giving them illumination of his word and his way. The citizens of the kingdom can get wisdom by way of revelation. These are things that the unbeliever will never gasp outside of the scope of God. That's the power of having mysteries unlocked because the Holy Ghost releases things that you need to function in whatever circumstance you may find yourself encountering. Revelation will give you perspective in a way that others in the world system can't see. In this vantage of perception, revelation is vitally important because it's God disclosing information that the people around you can't access. This is key because while others are concerned about the problem, God has already given you the solution. As a byproduct, you become the answer to another person's problem by being able to access revelation. That's why the soil of your mind has to be right and saturated by the Holy Spirit to cause it to be fertile enough to receive what God will release by way of revelation. You can't gain revelation with an immature mindset. I draw this point from Paul in 1 Corinthians 3:2. Paul tells the church at Corinth that I gave you milk, not solid food, for you were not ready for it, and you're still not ready. He says in essence that I can only give you revelation on the level of your ability to digest it. That's connected to the mind. The ability to understand and comprehend revelation. When your mindset is on milk, then it needs to be matured to be able to receive revelation that it can digest. Most of the problems in our lives are that we have a real need for maturity. Only maturity will change perception. Let's be open to having a changed mindset so that God can trust us with the mysteries of the kingdom.

CHAPTER 3

THE GRASSHOPPER EFFECT

Numbers 13:30-33 (NIV)

30 Then Caleb silenced the people before Moses and said, "We should go up and take possession of the land, for we can certainly do it."

31 But the men who had gone up with him said, "We can't attack those people; they are stronger than we are."

32 And they spread among the Israelites a bad report about the land they had explored. They said, "The land we explored devours those living in it. All the people we saw there are of great size.

33 We saw the Nephilim there (the descendants of Anak come from the Nephilim). We seemed like grasshoppers in our own eyes, and we looked the same to them."

I have been endeavoring to help us understand this great theme of perception. That God uses the eyes to get to the mind to train the mind how to think spiritually in spite of what we see in the flesh. We are humans with many limitations. In the area of perception, we only process information from a limited frame of reference. Our process of interpretation of the things that we collectively see will vary based on our frame of reference. The reason being is that we all have a different awareness because we have different backgrounds and come from different environments, so our factors for interpretation are not the same. Compared to God, he is omniscient. The divine attribute of perfect knowledge. The perfect knowledge of God is exclusively His attribute. It relates to Himself and all beyond Himself. It includes all things that are actual and all things that are possible. Its possession is incomprehensible to us, and yet it is necessary to our faith in the perfection of God's sovereignty. The revelation of this divine property like that of others is well calculated to fill us with profound reverence. The reason this is important information for us is that if God has perfect knowledge, then I can conclude, God is trying to train how I see and think so that he can train my reaction to what I see and think on another level. I think that for many of us, we haven't tapped into potentially all God has for us because we think too low, and so we see at the thinking level. If your thinking is low, then your vantage of perception will be equally as low. God has perfect knowledge of what will happen in all of our lives, so when God declares what will be, he isn't making an educated guess. He is revealing to us his perfect knowledge and his ability to warn us of what will come so that we can be prepared and see it the way God sees it, so no matter what happens, we will respond like people of faith. Faith then becomes the necessary component to my relationship with God because when I am faced with trials and tests, my perception is limited because I base my interpretation of life events on my own senses. God, who has perfect knowledge, already knows the end from the beginning. We have to be careful that we see right because the enemy will fool us. In every situation, there are many paths to take to get to an end, but that doesn't always mean the path that we take is the will of God for us. That's why I need to rely on trust in God so that I can see with the perception of faith. God tells us to trust Him and not to rely on our own understanding (Prov. 3:5,6). Why? Because He alone knows what He is doing and why. I certainly don't have an accurate or perfect knowledge of all things - or even any single thing. And this is where faith should come into play, reaching beyond our own limitations and placing our trust in the One who has no limitations. Faith, according to Holman Dictionary, is Trusting commitment of one person to another, particularly of a person to God. Faith is the central concept of Christianity. One may be called a Christian only if one has faith. It's faith that connects us to God in the first place.

This is the issue in this text of the 12 spies who Moses sent to spy out the land. The mission was to go and spy out the land that God said he was GOING to give them. Moses gave it special emphasis here because it was near Hebron that God had promised to give Abraham the land (Gen. 13:14-18). From there, Abraham had set out to defeat a coalition of kings (Gen. 14:13). The only piece of real estate Abraham possessed in Canaan was in Hebron, and there he and the other patriarchs lay buried. The spies, of course, knew these historical facts, and memories of these patriarchal events should have strengthened their faith in God as they passed through Hebron. Their commission had been to view the land and to report back on what they saw. It was not their job to determine if the Israelites could overcome the Canaanites. God had promised that He would give the land to His people. I think this is a good place to tell that you need to be careful that you don't let other people's bad perception hinder you from trusting in God. Sometimes people will force their minds on you because of the context that they came from, and because they are struggling with their faith, they will make you question the validity of the promise that God has made for you. I refuse to live my life under the perception of somebody else's context. It's critical because of the negative attitude that we all will transfer into our thinking. Negative thinking will absolutely ensure that you are already defeated. On a thinking level, negative thoughts have a greater impact on the brain than positive thoughts. It will affect decisions, conduct, and relationships. When people have negative perceptions, then they dwell on events that only reveal the negative. Their perception only allows them to register the bad in every situation. When we let others infiltrate our perception, they then gain the power to alter our self-esteem. Self-esteem is our opinion of ourselves, based on others' perceptions. That's why it's important that we are defined by the standards of God and not the negativity of man. This is the plight of the Israelites.

We see that the 10 spies come back and say they are too strong for us and we can't do it. They spread a bad report around the camp, and they made this declaration in verse 32, And they spread among the Israelites a bad report about the land they had explored. They said, "The land we explored devours those living in it. All the people we saw there are of great size. We saw the Nephilim there (the descendants of Anak come from the Nephilim). We seemed like grasshoppers in our own eyes, and we looked the same to them." One of their issues was that they had a poor self-image. They said we seem like grasshoppers in our own eyes. Self-image is related to what you see when you look in a mirror —

21

however, it goes much deeper than that. Self-image refers to how we see ourselves on a more global level, both internally and externally. "Self-image is how you perceive yourself. There are a number of self-impressions that have built up over time. These self-images can be very positive, giving a person confidence in their thoughts and actions, or negative, making a person doubtful of their capabilities and ideas." We see this negative side in the text when they say that we can't do it! They are stronger and taller than us. Self-image has a lot to do with self-esteem. After all, how we see ourselves is a big contributing factor to how we feel about ourselves. When my self-image is not where it needs to be, then it affects how I feel about myself, and as a byproduct, it affects how I perform in life. Then it has the proclivity to control how I see God because for some people; they see God on the level that they see themselves. They start to feel that God can't use them because of what they are not, but you have to remember that God is not like men. He doesn't call us and make promises to us based on where we have previously been, but he knows where we are going. Sometimes we have to remind ourselves that if God has made you a promise, then God has already factored in what you don't have and where you have been in relation to the past. Israel, as well as many of us, have to see that God has already given them the land. Why are you letting your poor image take precedence over the promise that God has already made? Having a negative self-image can certainly influence what we addressed before, and that is self-esteem; and having low self-esteem is likely to be accompanied by a negative self-image, but they are at least somewhat independent "self" aspects. Identity is also a closely related concept but is also a larger and more comprehensive one than self-image. Identity is our overall idea of who we are. Roy

Baumeister says, "The term 'identity' refers to the definitions that are created for and superimposed on the self." In other words, identity is the whole picture of who we believe we are — and who we tell ourselves and others that we are — while self-image is one piece of that picture. We can tell by the way these 10 spies are talking about how they view themselves because they call themselves what nobody else even said, and that was; we are like GRASSHOPPERS. Be careful that you don't hinder your own success by giving yourselves labels that don't fit your destiny. God calls us the head and not the tail. Above only and not beneath. He calls us blessed going in and blessed coming out. He calls us a city that is set on a hill that can't be hidden. He calls us prosperous; Royal priesthood and chosen nations. We have to be careful and aware that we have the perception of ourselves that God has given to us. They reveal their image of themselves by saying we are like grasshoppers. How do you view yourself? Some of us don't need people to call us names and destroy our view of ourselves because many of us do it from the inside. It's kind of like Naomi in the book of Ruth 1. She has been ravaged by life after losing her husband and sons, and now all she has is her daughter-in-law Ruth, and when they return home to Bethlehem, they ask the question, is that Naomi? She replies, don't call me Naomi, but call me Mara, which means bitter. She let her trauma change her perception of who she was. Just like Naomi, the children of Israel's words reveal their perception of themselves. We are like Grasshoppers! Not only that, then they deflect their self-image on an enemy that doesn't even know they are there. We seemed like grasshoppers in our own eyes, and we looked the same to them." How did they deduce what the enemy thought about them, and they hadn't talked to them? The answer that self-image also deals with the way a person interprets others' perceptions or what he thinks others think of him/herself. Their poor image of themself presupposed that the enemy thought of them the same way.

Their words also reveal another thought I think bears looking into, and that is the theme of being pessimistic. By definition, pessimism is the tendency to see, anticipate or emphasize only bad or undesirable outcomes, results, conditions, and problems. Pessimism hinders optimism. You can't have a favorable outcome when your perception is diluted by pessimistic thoughts. For the pessimist, if things are going right, then the perception is that it's too good to be true, and then they start to expect things to get worse, and as a result, you tend to open up the door to a level of fear that releases negative manifestation. We actually see this theme in the book of Job. In Job 3:25, he said that the thing that I feared has overtaken me, and what I dreaded has happened to me. It suggests that he had a secret fear that ended up producing the manifestation of his secret thoughts. Be aware that the negative thoughts can produce a negative manifestation. I have seen this in my own life. There have been times I let my negative thought life create the reality of my life. I have had trust issues that have been produced by past trauma, and I projected those negative feelings on everyone and everything around me. As a result, I always ended up getting what I expected, and that was negative. I had to change my thoughts and perceptions. When I did that, then I refused to allow the past traumatic experiences to dictate how I was going to see. I had to make the choice that even in what looks bad, God had already made a promise in Romans 8:28 that all things would work together for the good to them that love the Lord and are chosen according to his purpose. I had to resolve that I had a future and that no matter what things look like in the area of perception, that God's promises override what I see. What you see is a smokescreen that the enemy will use to mess with your perception. God promised that the bad and the good will still work for you when you learn how to see right. Some of us need to pray and ask God to help us see how he sees. Lord, give me your eyes. Help me to view my world how you view it and understand that God is working on our behalf even when the situation tries to tell me something different. In those moments, we have to resolve to let God be true and everything else a liar. Your negative situation is a liar.

Here is the prescription for the grasshopper effect. Remember the promise over the obstacle. They were looking at the giants, the land, and their own ability. God knew all of that before he ever promised them the land, but in spite of what things looked like around them, God made them a promise, and the God of the promise already worked out the particulars before they got there. That's why before you ever got into the situation, God had already worked out the situation on your behalf. We just have to trust him with the outcome and know that God is able to protect us and keep his promise. When you don't have that perception, you give up without a fight. How many of your dreams have died after God has already promised you that it will live? It didn't die because of God. It died because of your inability to trust the promise and step into it. For some of you, I think you need to revisit the promises that have been declared over your life and go back and revisit the dreams and aspirations that God has promised you. Reawaken those things and step into them with an optimistic faith that won't allow you to give up. For others, we have to rehearse the promise even in times where things get rough and throwing in the towel seems like the better option. In those times, remember that the obstacles don't negate the promise. The promise is already intact. What we have to do is make it to the spot of the promise. The next thing in this prescription is the size of the promise doesn't diminish the power of God to perform it.

The children of Israel were worried about the size of everything around them. From the land to the people, but size doesn't matter to God. No matter how big a thing can be, it doesn't worry God. God has the power to allow you to overcome every obstacle. Nothing is too big for his power to overcome. We even see this in the life of a young shepherd boy named David when he encountered a giant named Goliath. David prophesied the outcome of the fight before he ever threw a stone. We have to remember that big things fall hard in front of the promises of God towards his children. God's promises are already done in the realm of the spirit. I think that is what we need to see as people of God. God speaks from eternity into time. In eternity there are a series of events that aren't connected to our earth realm time. In eternity whatever God has proposed is already done there, and we are waiting for Kairos (God's time) to meet Chronos (earthly time). Don't let your poor perception hinder your success. What you see can hinder the go get it in you. If you don't get your perception correct, then it will cause you to see a situation as impossible when it's very possible if you go for it. We have to learn how to take the risk and trust God for the results. Joshua and Caleb in the text are key figures for what it means to have the right perception. In spite of the negative report that was given from the naysayers, Joshua and Caleb respond and say that we are well able. I want to tell you that you need people around you that can see the promises of God the way you see them. Like perceptions are key. You need people who can say together WE CAN DO THIS! If God has promised that it's ours, then it doesn't matter who is in the land. If God said it's ours, then somehow, we believe that God will move every obstacle out of the way. In fact, I believe that God made the promise and then showed them what was in the land to see if they would still trust Him in spite of. Hold on to the promise no matter what and watch God change things around you.

CHAPTER 4

WHAT'S DRIVING YOUR DECISIONS

Genesis 13:1-12 (NASB)

¹ So Abram went up from Egypt to the Negev, he and his wife and all that belonged to him, and Lot with him.

² Now Abram was very rich in livestock, in silver and in gold.

³ He went on his journeys from the Negev as far as Bethel, to the place where his tent had been at the beginning, between Bethel and Ai,

⁴ to the place of the altar which he had made there formerly; and there Abram called on the name of the LORD.

⁵ Now Lot, who went with Abram, also had flocks and herds and tents.

⁶ And the land could not sustain them while dwelling together, for their possessions were so great that they were not able to remain together.

7 And there was strife between the herdsmen of Abram's livestock and the herdsmen of Lot's livestock. Now the Canaanite and the Perizzite were dwelling then in the land.

8 So Abram said to Lot, "Please let there be no strife between you and me, nor between my herdsmen and your herdsmen, for we are brothers.

9 "Is not the whole land before you? Please separate from me; if to the left, then I will go to the right; or if to the right, then I will go to the left."

10 Lot lifted up his eyes and saw all the valley of the Jordan, that it was well watered everywhere – this was before the LORD destroyed Sodom and Gomorrah – like the garden of the LORD, like the land of Egypt as you go to Zoar.

11 So Lot chose for himself all the valley of the Jordan, and Lot journeyed eastward. Thus, they separated from each other.

12 Abram settled in the land of Canaan, while Lot settled in the cities of the valley, and moved his tents as far as Sodom.

Every day of our lives, we have to deal with the amalgamation of decisions. Big decisions. Small decisions. Life, in general, is a summation of choices and decisions that we have made. What to wear? What to eat? What career path? How many children to have? Who to date? Who to marry? What church to attend? When we are faced with some decisions, we might be tempted to just flip a coin and let chance determine our fate. In most cases, we follow a certain strategy or series of strategies to arrive at a decision point. There is a multitude of ways to decide. There is a model in psychological circles called the Single-Feature Model approach. It involves hinging your decision solely on a single feature. Imagine that you are buying rice. Faced with a wide variety of options at your local superstore, you decide to base your decision on price and buy the cheapest type of rice available. In this case, you ignored other variables (such as scent, brand, reputation, and effectiveness) and focused on just a single feature to decide. Then there is another model called Additive Feature Model. This method involves taking into account all the important features of the possible choices and then systematically evaluating each option. This approach tends to be a better method when making more complex decisions. Then there is what's called the Elimination by Aspects Model. The elimination by aspects model was first proposed by psychologist Amos Tversky in 1972. In this approach, you evaluate each option one characteristic at a time, beginning with whatever feature you believe is the most important. When an item fails to meet the criteria you have established, you cross the items off your list of options. Your list of possible choices gets smaller and smaller as you cross items off the list until you eventually arrive at just one alternative. Although there is a myriad of ways to make decisions, I want to argue in this chapter the issue of making decisions in your Flesh vs. your Faith.

We read the story of Abram, and we see the instructions that God told him to get out of his father's house and away from his kindred and pack his family and go to a land that God said I will show you. Abram obeyed the word of God and packed his family and set out. The bible says that he took with him his nephew Lot, who really was not attached to the instruction. As a side note, let me say this. Be careful that you don't add problems to your journey by taking people with you that don't belong. Sometimes we have to resolve that everybody we want to go on the trip with us might just be more of a burden than a blessing. We can add more load to the journey by adding weights that are not necessary to the destiny that God has established. Don't add more numbers to the equation than God planned on adding.

Abram treated Lot like a son more than a nephew. The issue with Lot is the issue many people face, and that is, Lot had no understanding or concern with spiritual matters. When you don't have an understanding of the matters of the spirit, then it only leaves you to the devices of the flesh. We actually see this contrast with Abram and Lot in the way they make decisions. The flocks and herds of both Abram and Lot increased so greatly that the land did not furnish enough pasture for the both of them, and consequently, disputes arose between their herdsmen. To put an end to strife, Abraham proposed separation and magnanimously left the choice of territory to his nephew, who selected the plain of Jordan and fixed his home at Sodom. According to the culture of this era Abram, as the head of the family household, has the right to choose first. Here lies the tension of the text. We see the character of Lot show up. This is the first look at Lots' carnality and love for the world showing itself in this passage. There were already a few things that were problematic because Abram and Lot are intelligent men, so I'm sure they knew there was an elephant in the room, and they saw that they both had too much wealth and herds between the two of them to stay together. Some of the conflicts that we have in our lives because of the inability to handle a potential problem before it arises. We neglect a lot of hard conversations and issues in our lives because we tend to think

31

that they will work themselves out. Maybe if we don't address it, it will get better. Many times, what is stressing us out and sending us through an emotional rollercoaster are the areas in our lives that we refuse to address head-on. God can't deliver what we deny. God will not solve for us what we will not confront ourselves. The truth with Abram and Lot is that no matter how much they wanted to stay together, no matter how close their relationship, they needed to separate. The arrangement that they had at the present moment was not going to work no matter what they tried to do. What's driving your decision to stay in something that's not working for you? Research has shown that when self-worth is not in a place where it needs to be, then we will settle for unsatisfactory relationships because we don't think that we can do any better. People tend to lower their expectations, so they don't expect much out of any relationship. The other thing for some is that we unrealistically see positive in people that really aren't there.

This passage reveals to us that a conflict between the workers of Abram and Lot was being waged over the best pastureland and water holes. Notice also that the conflict was not between Abram and Lot; it was only between their laborers. The two men had not yet been drawn into the conflict; their relationship had not yet been affected. Meaning that Abram was wise enough to know that petty arguments and conflicts eventually affect everyone unless they are dealt with in the beginning. When you have the right perception of things going on in your life, you learn how to address the foreseen before it becomes something bigger. How much better would our lives be if we learned that problems don't just work themselves out? How much better would the quality of our lives become when we learn that we have to be intentional to resolve conflict. Abram and Lot were about to become a poor testimony to the world. If you study this passage, you will discover that the Canaanites and Perizzites were living in the same area. This means these groups of people were watching the conflict between the workers of Abram and Lot, probably wondering how the two large ranchers would solve the problem. It was just a poor testimony for men of the true God to allow a situation to exist that would cause severe conflict. We have to be conscious that we realize that the world is watching us as children of God. How we handle each other matters to the world that is watching us. It's a poor indictment when the world handles conflict better than the people of God. We often overlook this perception in our culture, and as a byproduct, we mirror the world in how we handle adversity. Our language and disposition are not always becoming of a believer of Jesus Christ. We must become cognizant of how we handle situations that arise in our lives that are put on the world stage.

There are different outcomes when we have different perceptions as it relates to decision making. Decisions made through the perception of faith look through the eyes of faith. The way Abram showed his faith was that he operated in generosity as a means to exercise his faith. Abram allows his faith to solve strife. Faith doesn't make decisions that are based on selfishness. Real faith is connected to denying self. When faith drives our decisions, then it will keep in fellowship with a brother or sister. Faith says that I refuse to have a relationship with God and not have fellowship with the people of God. Faith says that I perceive you how God does. The typical issue for many people in the church community is that we think that our relationship with God has nothing to do with other human interaction. What we negate is that our dealings with people becomes the substratum of our relationship with God because that should drive my motives on how I handle others. You can't consistently damage people and claim allegiance to God. You can't be comfortable intentionally harming others with your attitude or your mouth and then saying that you love God. The Bible asks this question. How can you love God whom you haven't seen and hate your brother who you see every day? The kingdom of God is about reconciliation and forgiveness.

Abram suggested the need for keeping the peace between them and their workers. They were brothers, and brothers should not fight; brothers should care for each other and look after each other. It was faith that fueled Abram's ability to handle the conflict and faith-fueled the decision for Abram to give up his right for the benefit of Lot. Abram said in verse 9, the whole land is before us, so you make a choice. Abram is demonstrating the willingness by faith to go the extra mile and resolve the conflict without thinking about himself, but rather, focusing on Lot. Abram had great faith in God. He had learned this lesson in the famine experience when he failed to trust God's provision and went down into Egypt for help. Abram had learned that God would take care of him. That God expected the true believer to trust Him in the midst of turmoil. Abram was now willing to seek God and His righteousness above everything else. He was willing to trust God to take care of him even if Lot acted selfishly and usurped Abram's rights, and chose the best pastureland for himself. Oftentimes we think people are getting over because they choose what looks best from the perception of the flesh, but they are blinded by the consequences of their poor choice.

Remember that when God is in the equation, no enemy can get over or prevail over you. For Lot, he chose the best pasture, but it was in a wicked place, and he ended up in more trouble because of the choice that he made.

Lot shows us the consequences of perception through the eyes of the flesh. Lot was misled by what looked good. This was the beginning of Lot's fall. The decision he now made altered his life forever. Lot became a tragic illustration of selfishness, greed, carnality, and worldliness. Lot "lifted up his eyes" to look for the best region of the land. Lot jumped at the chance to get the best region. The idea is that he *immediately* lifted up his eyes and began to survey the land to see where the most watered and fertile region were. This should not have been the first thing he did, but it was. Lot was selfish and greedy. He should have "lifted up his eyes" to Abram, the man of God and the head of the family and insisted that he choose first. But Lot did not do this; in fact, there is no record that he even thanked or showed appreciation to Abram for the privilege of choosing first. Lot simply "lifted up his eyes" and immediately began to survey the land, looking for the very best land to claim. Lot had the perception of selfishness. He just wanted the very best for himself even though the right to choose first belonged to Abram. Flesh decisions always expose the condition of the mind and the heart. Bad perception shows itself in bad decisions, and behavior follows those decisions. Hey Lot! Remember that Abram took you in when he didn't have to. He took care of you and protected you, and when you had the opportunity to show some gratitude, you only considered yourself first. How, like so many people today, even children. Too many of us are selfish. We want the best for ourselves even if we have to neglect our parents and those who have helped us so much in life. Too many of us are unthankful and show little appreciation to those who have made us what we are. Be careful how you make your decisions because they will determine if you succeed or if you fail in your life and endeavors.

Here is food for thought before deciding.

1. Be careful of the motives that drive the decisions.

    People move for all kinds of reasons: seeking a better position, job, scenery, more money, a larger house, and on and on the reasons could go. When believers move, they must always look at the spiritual impact of the move. What will this decision bring about? Blessings or more unnecessary pain and issues.

2. We must check our perception of the decision. In other words, we must make sure that we can see from all angles. We must never be misled by appearance, by the lust of the eyes, and by what looks good. There is far more to life than the physical and material, far more than the bright lights, pleasures, possessions, positions, and wealth of this world. The things of this world do not satisfy the human soul: they leave the soul empty, dissatisfied, and unfulfilled. The only thing that satisfies the human soul is God and the things of God, things such as purpose, meaning, and significance; things such as love, joy, peace, goodness, faith, discipline, and control. The fullness of life comes only from God and from God alone; therefore, the major decisions of life must be made in light of God.

3. We must always consider God in the decision. We have to keep a watch on the impact that it will have on our spiritual growth if we make this decision.

CHAPTER 5

WE ARE NEVER IN THE DARK

2 Kings 6:8-14 (NIV)

8 Now, the king of Aram was at war with Israel. After conferring with his officers, he said, "I will set up my camp in such and such a place."

9 The man of God sent word to the king of Israel: "Beware of passing that place, because the Arameans are going down there."

10 So the king of Israel checked on the place indicated by the man of God. Time and again Elisha warned the king, so that he was on his guard in such places.

11 This enraged the king of Aram. He summoned his officers and demanded of them, "Will you not tell me which of us is on the side of the king of Israel?"

12 "None of us, my lord the king," said one of his officers, "but Elisha, the prophet who is in Israel, tells the king of Israel the very words you speak in your bedroom."

13 "Go, find out where he is," the king ordered, "so I can send men and capture him." The report came back: "He is in Dothan."

¹⁴ Then he sent horses and chariots and a strong force there. They went by night and surrounded the city.

I believe God is always at work on our behalf. He is working on our behalf to make sure that we are connected to him and that we are in the know as it relates to having proper information. It's not the will of God that we, as His people, walk around in a state of spiritual or revelatory ignorance. It's in the will of God that at every twist or turn of our lives that we have prophetic insight. In Hosea 4:6, we discover that God's people perish because of a lack of knowledge because they reject the knowledge. It's not because knowledge was withheld. God keeps his children in the know, especially his prophets. In Amos 3:7, the bible tells us that God does nothing on the earth unless he reveals it to His servants, the prophets. All throughout history, God has used the prophet to reveal his mind, but also, they would pick up what was going on in the world. God uses his prophets by opening up a spiritual portal in their minds and downloading things that others wouldn't be able to pick up. What seems to be lacking in this age is a prophetic voice. A mouthpiece for God that is open and listening for the voice, the rhythm, and the pace of God. We have been taught to shun and avoid the spooky, the mystical, and the weird, but the truth is we need a prophetic voice. We need a voice that will be able to tap into the mysteries of God. We need a voice that will be willing to go against the status quo of the day and speak out against the things that the normal person doesn't want to go against. We need a voice that isn't worried about being liked by men and known just on the earth, but a person that God can use, and their name is known in heaven. I want to warn and admonish you to get around people that God is talking to. Get around people that have an ear to the, more than just a person who knows the latest gossip around town. You need to surround yourself with seeking people. A people who long to know the will of God and the mysteries of God. Never surround yourself with people who are comfortable and stagnant. God will use his vessels to keep you grounded. He will use a vessel to warn you that you're around snakes. That you are moving too fast, and that isn't the will of God for you. YOU NEED A PROPHETIC VOICE. You need a prophet to shake you out of the mundane. You need a prophet to shift your thinking. You need a prophet to refocus you. You need a prophet who can instruct you on your next move. The truth is prophets don't preach what is popular. Neither do they preach to be popular. They often preach a truth that makes them unpopular. They are not owned by people and organizations; they are owned only by God. The prophet is devoted to God and truth, not institutions, organizations, religions, doctrines, and creeds. You need a prophetic voice!

This particular text is profound because if we are not careful, we will assume the main character of this drama is the prophet Elisha, but as in all scripture, the main character is the Lord. By what he said and did, as well as by what he didn't do, Elisha revealed the character of the God of Israel to King Joram and his people. God is using the prophet to show that Jehovah is not like the pagan idols. Our God keeps us in the loop because our God is a speaking God. Whenever the Syrians planned a border raid, the Lord gave Elisha the information, and he warned the king. Baal could never have done this for King Joram. The Lord sees not only the actions of people but also their thoughts and their hearts. I think that is a great place to remind us that nothing gets past the watchful eye of the Lord, who sees all and knows all and monitors all. That which others don't see because they can't see, God already knows. The king of Syria was sure there was a traitor in his camp, for the mind of the unbeliever interprets everything from a worldly viewpoint. The king is in paranoia because, as far as he knows, the only people that know what's going on are the people that are in the camp while they plan. Idolaters become like the gods they worship, so Ben Hadad was as blind as his god Rimmon. However, one of Ben Hadad's officers knew what was going on and informed the king that the prophet Elisha was in charge of "military intelligence" and knew what the king said and did even in his own bedroom. That's why you need a prophetic voice, but even more than that, that's why we ourselves need a relationship with the true God, because God will reveal to you the plots of your enemy, and while your enemy thinks you're ignorant, they don't know God has already revealed a way of escape. I can't tell you how many times God warned me about people and their plans and even things that were said behind the scenes that I wasn't privy to. When you serve God and work for him, God won't have you ignorant of the enemy's tactics and plots. God will prepare you by giving you information that other people aren't privy to. Before the enemy could make a move, God would download the information to his prophet. THERE IS NO SUCH THING AS SECRET INFORMATION WITH GOD! Some things you don't have to investigate. You don't have to go looking for information. Oftentimes God will tell you what you need to know, but you have to have faith enough in him to believe what he shows you. Most people are shocked by other people's actions, not because it actually happens, but if you tell the truth, God showed you that before it happens. The major shock is that God prepared you before it happened, but you blew it off as if you were tripping. God supernaturally reveals plots. I need to put some of your minds at ease by sharing with you that God knows when and how to show you what you don't know, but also God will protect you from the things he doesn't show you. There are some things that God knows that we can't handle.

The young man was an early riser, which speaks well of him, but we will see by his reaction that he was still deficient in his faith. Seeing the city surrounded by enemy troops, he did the normal thing and turned to his master for help. This young man had a perception issue. He based his emotions on what his physical eyes revealed. He did what any person with a poor perception would do, and that is panic. Panic is a sudden rush of fear and anxiety. The level of fear experienced is unrealistic and out of proportion to the events or circumstances that trigger the panic attack. He is unnerved and fearful because he thinks that what he physically sees in all there was, and that the outcome was going to be destruction. All this young man sees is a vast army. All he is thinking is we are about to die. Never let your physical sight cloud the vision of your spiritual eyes. God has given the believer another set of eyes that can see past what is on the surface. We have a sight that can see into the realm of the spirit, and God has a way of allowing us to see what is around us in the natural and then giving us peace in the midst of the storm. When I was growing up, I always loved the cartoon ThunderCats. The leader of the ThunderCats was Lion O, and he had a sword that would sense danger around him and warn him. Lion O would grab the sword and say," Give me sight beyond sight!" That's what we have in the realm of the spirit. We have the ability to see beyond. Isaiah 12:2 says,

"Behold, God is my salvation; I will trust, and not be afraid." When you perceive God right, then you know who he is in your life, and nothing you see can shake your faith. I have unshakable faith because I know that no matter what is coming up against me, I trust that God will bring me out, so I refuse to be dominated by my emotions that try to cause my mind to fear. Deuteronomy 20:3-4 may have come to mind where it says, "Do not let your heart faint, do not be afraid...for the Lord your God is He who goes with you, to fight for you against your enemies, to save you." That's why you have to always have a life of word meditation. The word of God has to always stay on your mind so that you can train your emotions to be controlled by the word and not by feelings. When you're in a chaotic situation, your reaction is everything. How you respond will determine the outcome. That's why you have to be full of the word and faith so that you can respond with the right perception. Elisha didn't trouble himself about the army; his first concern was for his frightened servant. If he were going to walk with Elisha and serve God, the young man would face many difficult and dangerous situations, and this meant that he had to learn to trust the Lord. Elisha understands that the servant's issue was a perception issue because when he comes to Elisha, he only speaks from the vantage of what he could physically see. Oftentimes in a crisis, God will give you a spiritual perception of heavenly protection. You have to be able to open those spiritual eyes and see it. The servant says to Elisha; these people are coming to kill us. What are we going to do? Elisha tells him, don't be afraid because those who are with us are more than them. The servant was living by sight and not by faith and couldn't see the vast angelic army of the Lord surrounding the city. The right perception of faith enables us to see God's hand at work, protecting us from what we can see as well as what we can't. Psalm 34:7 tells us, "The angel of the Lord encamps around those who fear Him and delivers them." The angels are servants to God's people, and until we get to heaven, we will never fully know how much they have helped us. There is an unseen army fighting for us to ensure us victory. They used to sing a song that says, all night and all day, angels keep watching over me. That's suggesting to us that God has never called us to battle without already dispatching the army of heaven to fight for us. Elisha said, my servant needs to know what I know and see what I see, so Lord, I need you to open his eyes. When God opened his eyes, he discovered that there was an army surrounding them all the time. I need to tell you that you are never alone! You might not understand it, but you have to grab hold to greater faith and understand that God has you covered. He covers who he calls! We are never in the dark! I like what God does in the story because Elisha prays again against the army as they are coming down, and blindness comes over the enemy. The servant who couldn't see in the spirit gets the right perception and sees what the enemy couldn't see. The enemy who had the plot got stricken with blindness. God will turn the tables on those who are against you; you just have to see it right!

CHAPTER 6

SEEING WHAT YOU HAVE

Ephesians 1:18-21 (MSG)

18 your eyes focused and clear, so that you can see exactly what it is he is calling you to do, grasp the immensity of this glorious way of life he has for Christians,

19 oh, the utter extravagance of his work in us who trust him – endless energy, boundless strength!

20 All this energy issues from Christ: God raised him from death and set him on a throne in deep heaven,

21 in charge of running the universe, everything from galaxies to governments, no name and no power exempt from his rule. And not just for the time being, but forever.

God has always had a plan from the beginning of time. The plan of God is always unfolding. That's one of the reasons we have to fully engage in the word of God because it contains the self-revelation of God, as well as the will of God, and God's dealings with man. When Adam and Eve rebelled, humans were separated from God because of sin. God's holiness required punishment and payment (atonement) for sin, which was eternal death. Our own death is not sufficient to cover the payment for sin. I always wondered if people understand what they were saying when they would say," It should have been me on the cross." If it were us, we would have just died. Only a perfect, spotless sacrifice, offered in just the right way, can pay for our sins. Jesus Christ, the perfect God-man, came to die on the cross to offer the pure, complete, and everlasting sacrifice to remove, atone, and make eternal payment for sin. The reason God did this is because he loves us. God loved us so much that he gave us his best gift, to be a sacrifice for us. God's plan of salvation has one goal, to connect God with his redeemed ones in the closest of relationships. The Lord of heaven and earth wants to walk with us, talk with us, comfort us and be with us through every experience of life. Allow me to give you a major truth; accepting God's offer of salvation won't solve all of our problems. It won't make life easier. Unfortunately, that is just one of many common misconceptions about the Christian life. But we will find a love that changes everything. We will also begin to experience a new kind of freedom that comes through the forgiveness of sin. Most people don't understand that God has a plan for their lives, so they walk around defeated. Some people are saved and love God but yet live beneath their privileges in Jesus because they don't have a revelation of what they have. I don't know of anything more crucial as a foundation to the Christian life than for the believer to see what has been completed for him 'in Christ Jesus'. We find the grace of God at work. A common definition is 'God's Riches At Christ's Expense.' Another definition is 'the unmerited favour of God.' Both of these are true definitions, but the one that I like the best is simply 'God's love set free.' You see, grace incorporates all that God desired to do for mankind because of His love, which He is now free to perform because His justice has been met through the sacrificial death of His son. So, in acting righteously because of the cross, God's love is now free to act as He will! And oh, how He has acted for the believer if only we could see it! There are no limits and restrictions on the love of God being poured out in our lives because we are in Christ.

Paul writes this letter to the Ephesian church to show them the union and unity of believers, and he is relating this unity and union both to Jews and Gentiles. With the revelation of this truth, Paul gives and discusses the position that we have in Christ. In most of Paul's letters, there is a sharp distinction drawn between what God has done for us by grace and how we are to live because of this fact of grace. The divine order that God has established through these letters is to first sit and learn of your position in Christ, and then, because of this position, the exhortation is given to live a life consistent with your position. In other words, the Christian life is becoming (in your experience) what you already are (in your position in Christ). Watchman Nee said:

"Most Christians make the mistake of trying to walk to be able to sit, but that is a reversal of the true order. Our natural reason says, If we do not walk, how can we ever reach the goal? What can we attain without effort? How can we get anywhere if we do not move? But Christianity is a strange or odd business! If at the outset we try to do anything, we miss everything. For Christianity begins not with a big DO, but with a big DONE. Thus, Ephesians opens with the statement that God has blessed us with every spiritual blessing in the heavenly places in Christ,' and we are invited at the outset to sit down and enjoy what God has done for us; not to set out to try and attain it for ourselves."

Paul talks about our position, and that deals with our legal status. When the Bible says that by faith in Christ, we are justified (declared not guilty), it is referring to our position. The biblical term 'justified' in reference to Christians has solely a judicial meaning. The issue that most of us have in the modern church is that they can't grasp in their minds that everything we need is already done in Jesus Christ.

We have discussed that perception deals with how you see a thing. It gives interpretation to what is going on in our world and how the stimuli in our minds relate to what we see. This is what perception is all about. When your perception is off, as it relates to God, and life, then interpretation about God and life is distorted. What Paul says to the Ephesian church is that I don't want you to have the wrong perception about your position in Christ. If you get that wrong, then your relationship with God will be based on the works and not on faith in the finished work of Jesus Christ. It needs to be emphasized that the benefits package that we have in Jesus Christ is not because we go to church. We don't go to church as a means to be saved. We go to church because we are saved, and we want to be around other believers in the community of faith. Paul wanted to encourage them to lay hold of the riches of God's grace in Christ. As Paul considers this, he breaks out in praise while he explains the gift that the believers have been given. He says, I pray that the eyes of your heart may be enlightened, so that you may know what the hope of His calling is, what are the riches of the glory of His inheritance in the saints. This says that if I'm going to see what I have in Christ, then I have to have the right perception of what I have in him.

Perception deals with the eyes. It is a synthetic process where different physiological and psychological processes are involved. For example, the accuracy of sense organs, clarity of sensations, mental set of an individual all play a role. Otherwise, our perception may go wrong. If the sight of the thing is off, then the understanding will also be off. Paul says I want you to know what you have in Christ, so I'm praying that you have your eyes fine-tuned. The word eye is the Greek word ophthalmos (of-thal-mos'), meaning the eye or vision. It's where we get the word ophthalmologist, which deals with the study and treatment of disorders and diseases to the eye. He says the eyes of your heart, though. Heart is the Greek word kardia. In most modern cultures, the heart is thought of as the seat of emotions and feelings. But most ancients — Hebrews, Greeks, and many others — considered the heart (Greek *kardia*) to be the center of knowledge, understanding, thinking, and wisdom. The New Testament also uses it in that way. The heart was considered to be the seat of the mind and will, and it could be taught what the brain could never know. The mind is connected to the soul. The brain is connected to the body. The brain is an organ. The mind is actually the place of operation. The mind and the brain aren't the same. The problem with many people is that we put feelings above knowledge. That's why it's difficult to give some people the authentic truth because their feelings will get in the way of the truth. We live in a culture that wants to create their own truth because they won't be held accountable for real truth that only comes from the word of God. That's why you get people who don't know the scripture but will tell you; I don't feel that is right because it doesn't sound right. Instead of their emotions being controlled by God's truth, their emotions distorted their understanding of His truth. You will never get the results God desires in your life without embracing the truth that God has revealed. We can't make our truth God's truth. That is to bring the word of God down to human limitations. I have to receive God's word as full authority in my life and then govern my life according to the truth that God has revealed. I need God to train my eyes so that I can have the right interpretation in my mind so that I can have powerful spiritual illumination.

Paul prays for the minds of the Ephesians to be enlightened. The Greek word for enlighten is phōtizō, which deals with illumination. It means to give light. Emotions have a significant place in the Christian life, but they are reliable only as they are guided and controlled by God's truth — which we come to know and understand through our minds. When the Holy Spirit works in the believer's mind, He enriches it to understand divine truth that is deep and profound and then relates that truth to life — including those aspects of life that involve our emotions. When the Holy Spirit brings us into revelation, that revelation is not just to be intellectual but to activate in the mind so that it can be applied. The proper application of divine illumination for the purpose of heart transformation. Sometimes we are so emotional that we are blinded from the truth. In Luke 24:31and 32, Jesus is walking with the two men on the Emmaus Road, their hearts (that is, their minds) burned within them; but it was not until their eyes were opened that they recognized Him. Before the Spirit enlightened them, they had the information but not the understanding; what they knew was true, but they could not, in the power of their own minds, grasp the meaning and significance of it. When Jesus gave them revelation of who he was before he left them, then they said did not our hearts burn within as he talked to us? I don't just want knowledge, but I need my mind to grab hold of the information so that I can have the ability to put it into practical application in my life. I need God to cut the light of illumination on my mind, so I can rest in the plan that he has for my life and walk in my calling. It's a dangerous thing to live a life with no revelation. The enemy always wants us in a state of ignorance to the word of God because inside the word lies the information, I need to unlock my destiny. Where there is no revelation, then there is no key to destiny. As a byproduct, we will exist and take up space but never step into all that we were designed to live for. I have to have the right perception of what I have. Then I need powerful illumination.

Finally, I want to address the fact that we need the right perception to embrace the benefit package that is outlined in the word of God. The apostle asks that they be given the understanding of the hope of His calling and the riches of the glory of His inheritance in the saints. He prays for God to enlighten them about the magnificent truths of election, predestination, adoption, redemption, forgiveness, wisdom, insight, inheritance, sealing, and pledge of the Holy Spirit.

Hope is the Greek word Elpis, which is expectation and confidence. Those truths summarize God's master plan for the redemption of mankind, His eternal plan to bring men back to Himself through His own Son, thereby making them His children. Now that they belonged to Christ by faith, Paul's supreme desire was for the Ephesian believers to fully realize what their new identity meant. "You were no afterthought of God. "God not only chose to save you, but He chose to save you before you existed before you would have the opportunity by His grace to choose Him. That is who you are!" In other words, I have to see right to understand my identity in Christ so that I can see what I have in him! I refuse to walk around as if I'm average any longer when I know I can embrace the benefit package that I have in Jesus and walk in victory in every situation that I face in life! Not another day should we be satisfied living beneath what God has intended. Get away from thinking that does not line up with the biblical definition of my identity. Get away from words that don't reflect the character of the definition that God has intended. I am who God says I am, and I have to see myself in that mirror of the word of God. In order to do that, I need the right perception.

CHAPTER 7

AFTER THIS YOU WON'T SEE ME THE SAME

Daniel 3:26-30 (NIV)

26 *Nebuchadnezzar then approached the opening of the blazing furnace and shouted, "Shadrach, Meshach and Abednego, servants of the Most High God, come out! Come here!" So, Shadrach, Meshach and Abednego came out of the fire,*

27 *and the satraps, prefects, governors and royal advisers crowded around them. They saw that the fire had not harmed their bodies, nor was the hair of their heads singed; their robes were not scorched, and there was no smell of fire on them.*

28 *Then Nebuchadnezzar said, "Praise be to the God of Shadrach, Meshach and Abednego, who has sent his angel and rescued his servants! They trusted in him and defied the king's command and were willing to give up their lives rather than serve or worship any god except their own God.*

29 *Therefore I decree that the people of any nation or language who say anything against the God of Shadrach,*

Meshach and Abednego be cut into pieces and their houses be turned into piles of rubble, for no other god can save in this way."

30 Then the king promoted Shadrach, Meshach and Abednego in the province of Babylon.

I think it is important that we come to a real mental understanding of the truth that all of us will, at someplace in life, face tough situations. It is an inevitable part of life and growth. The difference between success and failure is the way you see it. If you view it as a means to grow and develop, you will ultimately find great success. If you get bitter, resentful, and complain, then you will wallow in failure.

Viktor Frankl was a Jewish psychiatrist who spent three years during World War II living under unspeakable circumstances in several of the most notorious Nazi concentration camps. While imprisoned, Frankl realized he had one single freedom left: He had the power to determine his response to the horror unfolding around him. And so, he chose to imagine. He imagined his wife and the prospect of seeing her again. He imagined himself teaching students after the war about the lessons he had learned. Frankl survived and went on to chronicle his experiences and the wisdom he had drawn from them.

"A human being is a deciding being," he wrote in his 1946 book, "Man's Search for Meaning," which sold more than 10 million copies. "Between stimulus and response, there is a space. In that space is our power to choose our response. In our response lies our growth and our freedom."

In the context of perception, we have to know that human perception and the ramifications of that perception are important as well as life-changing. All of our perceptions can be subjected to interpretation. When it comes to perception -- seeing, feeling, hearing, and sensing things -- there is no such thing as objectivity. As humans, we have evolved to make sense of things. Every time a stimulus comes to us, our brain does the efficient thing: It responds based on past experiences. In doing so, the brain continually redefines normality. It is being shaped, literally, as a consequence of trial and error. The brain did not evolve to see the world the way it really is. We can't help but see things according to history. Our history and that of our ancestors because we are defined by ecology. Ecology is the branch of biology that deals with the relations of organisms to one another and their physical surroundings. Not by our biology, not by our DNA, but by our history of interactions.

For example, I used to spend the summer with my cousin, and she was infamous for making her famous beans. We would eat them so much, and because of these past experiences, to this very day, I loathe the thought of beans. My wife wanted to make them for me a few times, and I got nauseous just thinking about it. It is because of the perception of my past experiences that I have drawn a mental interpretation that I don't like beans. What really matters in the realm of perception is what we do with the information that we perceive. The greatest issue we have is that we don't perceive our trials right, so the way we interpret the information is the reason we can't progress in life and in God. God uses trials for development and not a disaster. He uses it to test our faith and grow us in the areas of our lives that are not as strong as they need to be. Then the other side of that is that God will use the story of our life to get a message to someone else. He wants to reveal to the people who are around you the God that you serve. That God will use situations in your personal life to change the perception of someone else to the God that you serve. Where there is no evolving perception, there is no breakthrough. For a true breakthrough to take place, there has to be a mind shift.

This biblical story reveals the issues that we face when we refuse to compromise our standards and jeopardize our faith in God. Anytime you refuse to follow the perceptions and mindset of the crowd and live a life submitted to God, there will always be a conflict. We, as people of God, have to be willing to hold fast to who we are amidst a people who will go along to get along. We have to be willing to make waves in the culture to make changes in the perception of the world and culture around us. Too many times, we are ok with the status quo because we don't want to feel as if we are making waves. I want to submit to you that God has called us to make waves in the culture. God never wanted us to blend in, but rather we have been called to stand out. It's ok to not be like the world. It's ok to have a biblical worldview and hold fast to the standards that the word of God prescribed for us to abide by.

When we deal with the background of this text, we discover that Nebuchadnezzar is faced with a problem because he has this vast empire that is filled with different cultures, languages, people, and groups of nationalities from Babylon to Egypt. He is trying to unify them so that they can function as one. What he does is come up with a state religion and wants the people to unify under the heading of this one religion that he himself will be the head of. He builds this golden image that he had in a dream years before, so he sets it up and tells everyone that when you hear the sound of the instruments, everyone is to bow down and worship the image that is set up. This would cause the true believers in God a real test. The issue is a matter of life or death because the ones that won't comply will be thrown into a fiery furnace to their death. There are a few takeaways I want to submit from this story that will help us in the area of perception.

One thing you have to realize is that your promotion can breed jealousy from other people. The text shows us that these astrologers, who are of Babylonian nationality, go to the King and says that these Jews that you have promoted aren't complying with the rules that you set up. It was their jealousy that fueled them to expose the Hebrew boys. They are upset with the fact that the King promoted some Jews over his own Babylonian blood. There is always a reason that people are looking to cause your downfall. If I were a betting man, I would bet that they are mad because of the favor that was on the Hebrew boys. The problem with jealousy is that it masks other feelings and attitudes that are even more hurtful to us and those closest to us. Its intensity is often shielding deep-seated feelings of possessiveness, insecurity, or shame. I believe that what lies at the heart of jealousy very often isn't the threat itself but a drive we have within us to torment ourselves and berate ourselves with self-critical thoughts. Jealousy is the suggestion that heaven has run out of resources to bless, so we have to want what someone else has.

The issue of jealousy is a perceived threat of any kind. That perception is predicated on the mentality of the person. If you don't perceive yourself in the right light, then you always think others are a threat to you because there is an inner voice that is inside of you that belittles you. This threat can be real or imagined. Some people are jealous of you because of something that they placed in their own minds about you that isn't true. Some people are jealous of you because of what they see you with, and they don't understand that you yourself are struggling to maintain what you have. That's why people say don't judge a book by its cover. I am amazed at people being jealous of other's giftedness and not understanding that the gift is a struggle for the gifted.

Jealousy can compel someone to obsessively monitor another's communication, relationships, and whereabouts, attempt to lower their self-confidence, or even behave violently. In this case, the only way the astrologers could see what was going on with the Hebrew boys was because they had to be monitoring them in an attempt to catch them doing wrong. You have to be careful because most times, when people are watching you, it's because they could be looking for a weakness in you to feed the jealousy in them because of what they are lacking personally.

Secondly, we have to resolve that our standards for God are nonnegotiable. The Hebrew boys had a resolve to stand for God! These three young men faced the ultimate test of their faith. They either had to disobey the Lord or disobey the king. And their decision was a matter of life or death. It was easy for the other officials of Babylon to declare their first loyalty to the state, for the crowd believed in many gods. The image representing the state of Babylon was merely another god to be added to the others that were worshipped throughout the empire. But not to these three men.

They believed in the Lord, the only living and true God revealed in the Scriptures. They knew Him in a very personal way, and when you really know God and what he can do for those who stand for him, then you're not moved by the dangers that come from being a servant of his. From the earliest days of childhood, all three of these young men had made the Word of God the center of their lives. Therefore, their first loyalty belonged to the Lord. When it came down to the King, they declared, we don't care how mad you are. We don't care about the consequences of these actions; we refuse to bow!

They declared you might think your god is bad, but the God we serve, he can deliver us. Because of our view of God being together and having the right perception of who he is, even if he doesn't, it wasn't because he couldn't. In other words, our faith in him is not up for debate. We are settled and resolved. Real faith in the ability and the character of God will put you in situations where you have to make hard choices. Right perception of God leads to the right decisions about what I believe about him.

Finally, when your faith is intact, then your victory will change the perception of your enemy about your God. Nebuchadnezzar witnessed the Lord's miraculous deliverance of Shadrach, Meshach, and Abednego. Having watched the soldiers catch fire and the three young men fall into the blazing furnace, the king was totally taken aback and utterly stunned by what he saw next. To make sure his eyes were not deceiving him, he asked the officials around him if they had not thrown three bound men into the fire. When the officials said yes, the king shouted, "Look! Now there are four men walking around in the furnace, unbound and completely unharmed by the blazing fire."

Nebuchadnezzar's description of the fourth man: he looked like a *divine being*. Although the fourth person was probably a pre-incarnate appearance of the Son of God, Nebuchadnezzar knew nothing about Christ. All he knew was that the person looked like a son of the gods. Approaching as close as he could to the blazing furnace, the king shouted out for Shadrach, Meshach, and Abednego to come out. Notice his acknowledgment that the men were servants of the most high God. When the three climbed out of the blazing furnace, the shocked officials crowded around to inspect them. Their bodies and clothes were not even singed. There was not even a smell of fire or smoke on them. All the officials of Babylon, including King Nebuchadnezzar himself, had just witnessed an astounding miracle. The Lord had proven that He is the only living and true God, far more powerful than the so-called gods of this world and the rulers who dare to defy Him.

No matter what you are going through in your life, you and I must never lose sight of the correct perception about God and his dealings with us. You being solid and firm in your faith is going to change the way someone else perceives God. Remember, God has put us on display to the world around us. Live well and go through well because we are coming out of our fiery furnace without a singe!

CHAPTER 8

WHEN SEEING ISN'T THE SAME

Numbers 13:30-33 (NIV)

30 *Then Caleb silenced the people before Moses and said, "We should go up and take possession of the land, for we can certainly do it."*

31 *But the men who had gone up with him said, "We can't attack those people; they are stronger than we are."*

32 *And they spread among the Israelites a bad report about the land they had explored. They said, "The land we explored devours those living in it. All the people we saw there are of great size.*

33 *We saw the Nephilim there (the descendants of Anak come from the Nephilim). We seemed like grasshoppers in our own eyes, and we looked the same to them."*

Someone has defined a committee as "a group of people who individually can do nothing and collectively decide nothing can be done." It is amazing how in anything, people can be on the same team and be looking at the same thing but perceive and interpret what they see in a variety of ways. It is always a danger to be around people, working with people, and worship people that have a negative impact on the way you think because they are trying to make decisions predicated on their own bad perception. Other people's bad mentality can infect the rest of the team. It can affect the ministry. It can affect the business. It can affect productivity in any area that you're trying to aspire.

If you don't have your own mind, then it becomes easy to fall prey to the negativity of others and then adopt the same thinking pattern. As a byproduct, you infect the production of what God has planned for you and the people connected to you. BAD THINKING CAN BE INFECTIOUS! It's a cancer and a silent killer to destiny and the dreams God has for you. I would admonish all of you, be aware that you don't fall into the trap of polluted thinking because of your bad company. Whoever has your ear has your mind. You can't afford to be around dream abortionists. People's pessimisms infecting your thoughts and hindering forward movement. You have to be willing to choose your destiny over some of your friendships. Don't be hindered by the mental infections of your circle.

Because they lacked faith, all the spies except Caleb and Joshua were discouraged at the prospect of entering the land and fighting the enemy, and their discouragement quickly spread throughout the camp. Doubt had turned into unbelief, and unbelief is rebellion against God. It's interesting how in Num. 13:27, the ten spies identified Canaan as "the land to which you sent us" and "the land through which we have gone" (v. 32), but not as "the land the Lord our God is giving us." Because these ten men were walking by sight, they didn't really believe God's promises. They looked at the people of the land and saw giants; they looked at the Canaanite cities and saw high walls and locked gates; they looked at themselves and saw grasshoppers.

The problem was not only a faith issue, but it was a faith issue that stemmed from poor perception. They were looking through the eyes of flesh and basing their interpretation of what they saw by their own ability to do, or not do, what God has promised. It is dangerous when you believe your own eyes over the promises of God. There will be times when God will give you a big promise and then test your perception of what he promised. Can you believe that God will work the details out even when you can't see it? Can you trust the promise and the process? I want to submit to many of you that what you see is not the denial of the promise but the test of perception. The 10 spies looked at themselves through their esteem lenses and concluded because it looks like the odds are too big for us that there is no way this can be the will of God. When your self-perception is faulty, then it's hard to move past your own inabilities to even fathom what God has said. For some reason, they let their anxiety about what they saw nullify the promise that God has already given them, and worse yet, they let that mentality spread.

You would think that as a people, Israel would have the right perception of God by now. This is the same God that brought them out of Egypt. This is the same God that delivered them from Pharaoh. This is the same God that said, I freed you so that you can worship me and be my people, and I'll be your God. They were people who had, up until this point, saw the mighty hand of God move for them in extraordinary ways. Yet, like many of us today, when they saw a situation that seemed bigger than they could handle, they forgot the promises of God because of their inward issues. Most of our real issues with faith and trusting God is that we believe that God will do certain things and he won't do other things. We are holding God hostage to the people on the earth that hurt you. Most of us are struggling with how can God keep his promises to me when I'm not worthy? We have to understand that God called Israel by his own providence. It was not that God didn't know what he was getting. This means that God knows what he is promising you before he ever told you, and he knew your problems before he gave you the promise. What you have to know is that no matter how big something may look to you; God is still ABLE! He is not a promise-breaker! God is not like your caregivers who made you promises and failed at times! Our God cannot lie!

I want to argue the two positions that I see in the text. You have 12 spies, and two of them said that we could do it, and 10 spies say that we can't because they were going on what they saw and not what God said. The first position I want to argue is Confidence. Right perception of God and his promises builds confidence. Confidence by those who study the subject is "the degree to which you think and "feel" your actions will achieve positive results." I always wondered why in the game of basketball, a player could be having a bad game, and they keep shooting? It's because when they know their ability, they have confidence that whenever they shoot a shot that it's going in, so they keep going even in the midst of a bad game. Be clear that confidence and self-esteem are not the same.

Self-esteem refers to general feelings about yourself; confidence refers to your belief and feeling that you can perform a task successfully. The better you feel about yourself, the easier it becomes to build confidence for a specific task. God is trying too, for many of us, to build our faith in him to the degree that it builds confidence in our ability to go get whatever God has said he was going to give us. The right perception and faith in the promises of God will cause you to tackle a task without trepidation. It doesn't matter how big the problem may be; if it goes against what God has promised me, then it has to move around. The catalyst to bring the function of confidence to life is the realization that your actions influence your results.

In other words, "it's up to you." If you do not believe in this assignment fully, you will not make an effort to do your best since the outcome is out of your control. Caleb and Joshua said, let's take it now because we can do it. In other words, I believe in what God told us that we could do and have. It built his confidence that we can defeat whoever is in the land no matter their size because we are able. The God kind of confidence will affect your perception that there is no such thing as defeat when it comes to what God has said!

Here again, we must drive the point home to avoid the infection of the pessimist. Pessimism can be described as a tendency to think negatively. A person who has pessimistic tendencies may frequently find and focus on the negative aspects of a situation rather than concentrating on the positive ones. Pessimism can refer to a fixation on the darker aspects of a situation or event, to the expectation of a negative outcome, or a lack of hope for the future. Those who tend toward pessimism may also feel helpless and believe that any actions taken are unlikely to have an impact on a negative outcome.

They may believe themselves to be passive agents in the world and largely attribute any chance of success to external factors that cannot be controlled. Typically, research has suggested that the pessimistic disposition comes from our environment that breeds us. That is, we were born and raised in a negative environment that the toxic mindset filtered down to us, and that is how we govern our lives. Bad experiences in our lives cause us to be pessimistic. If all we are accustomed to is failing, then we can adopt the attitude that nothing will go our way.

The children of Israel were that way because they were always complaining every time a bad situation came about. When they were at the Red Sea, and Pharaoh was behind them, they cried out in fear and talked about how they should have never left Egypt. Poor company is another reason. I am sure you have met at least one pessimistic person who never failed simply because he never tried anything!! Pessimism isn't only caused by bad past experiences, but it can result from listening to people who tell you about their bad past experiences. If you are surrounded by pessimists, then you will certainly become one after some time, even if you never failed before. The 10 spies said we can't do it! They didn't even want to try because they were judging the situation on what they saw instead of what God promised, and it started to affect the rest of the people. Numbers 13:32 (NIV) And they spread among the Israelites a bad report about the land they had explored. They said, "The land we explored devours those living in it. All the people we saw there are of great size.

How do we handle a pessimistic attitude?

1. Highlight the positives in your life. For the children of Israel, they had the promise and the proven faithfulness of God in the past to focus on. If the 10 spies had thought about all the good things that God has already done, they would have learned that these giants in the land were only another opportunity for God to show himself powerful in their lives.

2. Keep things in perspective. We all have to learn that some things can appear to be a setback. In those moments, remember what you know about God and his dealing with you in the past. Every time the people of God came up against a situation that threatened what God told them, he always stepped in and made a way.

3. Hang out with optimistic people. The company we keep matters. It's human to want to fit in. If we hang out with people who always find the cloud around a silver lining, our natural tendency is to do the same. If we look for people who are cheerful doers, we will likely soak in the positivity and see reasons to be cheerful, too.

I've heard it said that optimistic people aren't paying attention. I counter that to really pay attention means to remember that everyday millions of people do millions of things that are ordinary and good and that give them joy. Caleb and Joshua were optimistic. They kept the promise in view, and they had the right perception about God and themselves. They said we got this!

CHAPTER 9

THE NEED FOR A MINDSET CHANGE

M any think that the only problem with the human mind is that it doesn't have access to all the knowledge it needs. The suggestion is that we need more education. So, education becomes the great instrument of redemption — personal and social. If people just got more education, they would not use their minds to invent elaborate scams, sophisticated terrorist plots, and complex schemes for embezzling. If people just got more education. The issue with that is that some people get more education with the sole intent to become smarter at doing wrong. If the mindset's motive is wrong, then the result will be educated wickedness.

The Bible has a far more profound analysis of the problem. In Ephesians 4:23, Paul uses a striking phrase to parallel Romans 12:2. He says, "Be renewed in the spirit of your minds. "The spirit of your mind." It means at least this: the human mind is not a sophisticated computer managing data, which is then faithfully presented to the heart for appropriate emotional responses.

The mind has a "spirit." In other words, our mind has what we call a "mindset." It doesn't just have a view; it has a viewpoint. It doesn't just have the power to perceive and detect; it also has a posture, demeanor, a bearing, an attitude, and a bent. "Be renewed in the spirit of your mind." The word spirit is a Greek word that has Holy Spirit implications that says that if my thoughts are not renovated or changed by the Holy Spirit, then it will be controlled by the flesh or under satanic control.

"The problem with our minds is not merely that we are finite, but that we are fallen." The problem with our minds is not merely that we are finite and don't have all the information. The problem is that our minds are in a fallen state. They have a spirit, a bent, a mindset that is hostile to God. Our minds are bent on not seeing God as infinitely more worthy of praise than we are or the things we make or achieve. We are so consumed with wanting to be the god of our own existence. We crave our own control, and we are bent on being the controlling factor in our lives. Sometimes even at our own detriment.

That's what's wrong with our minds. This illumines the relationship between verses 1 and 2 of Romans 12. Verse 1 says that we should present our bodies — that is, our whole active life — as a living sacrifice, which is our spiritual service of worship. So, the aim of all life is worship. That is, we are to use our bodies — our whole lives — to display the worth of God and all that he is for us in Christ. Now it makes perfect sense when verse 2 says that, in order for that to happen, our minds must be renewed.

That suggests that the mind is the key to transformation. Our minds are not by nature God-worshipping minds. They are by nature self-worshipping minds. That is the spirit of our minds. Renewing our minds is not simply "changing" our thoughts but actually putting off the old, negative thoughts and replacing them with the mind of Christ. In other words, we can't just say to God, "Lord, give me Your Thoughts," and somehow expect Him to "automatically" give us His Mind. We must first put off our own self-centered thinking by confessing, repenting, and then giving it to God. At this point, we can then put on the Mind of Christ. The issue with most of our mentality is that it is set based on our own preferences and biases. We are social in our thinking. We have the innate need to belong and to be called normal according to the standards of the world, that we have failed to realize that the kingdom was never designed to be normal. It's supposed to be set apart. That says that what the world calls normal is abnormal to the citizens of the kingdom, and until we understand that we need to get out of the social mind in order to embrace the kingdom mind, we won't transform. We might be in the world, but we are not governed by this world system.

Transform is the Greek word metamorphoō. We see a derivative of this word on the mount of transfiguration where Jesus was hanged into another form. That's what transformation is about. It's changing into another form. To have a mind transformation means that my mind has to change into another form. It's not about all the externals that we think. We tend to believe that if I change on the outside, I'm changed on the inside, but that is not true. Our mind dictates everything about us. I have to have a mindset reset. My mind has to be baptized in the Holy Ghost so that he can clean all the impurities out of my brain and replace it with the ability to think like God. It's the will of God that we have his thinking pattern.

That says that for some people, you have to do spiritual spring cleaning. Declutter your mind. Get rid of the thought patterns that have been messing up your life. That could mean for some that we have to get toxic people and things out of our minds and do a spiritual cleansing on the way we have been letting our minds run. We have to even reinvent ourselves mentally. We ascribe reinventing ourselves to outward looks, but I want to suggest that we need to reinvent the way our thoughts run out of control. We have to learn how to let the word of God dictate the movements of the mind. A mental overhaul is in order.

Get rid of things that are consuming your time and energy that aren't necessary. For some, it's those everyday things that can distract us, like how we handle life and life's struggles. Life happens to all of us whether we are saved or unsaved. The difference between the kingdom and the world is how we engage the issues that we face. The word has a remedy for every problem, but we have to acknowledge that the world has a remedy as well. The remedy of the world goes against the mindset of God. The world wants a quick fix, but those of us in the kingdom understand that sometimes it is a test of our faith. That's why when you have a transformed mind, you don't panic and throw tantrums because of what you face. We learn how to trust God and depend on him. Now that doesn't suggest that we aren't human, and we don't have moments. It means that even when I'm faced with a reality that I don't like; I'm still resolved to trust in God. When you trust God on that level of mental mindset change, then all I need from God is my next step into the future. Then I trust God that he will order every subsequent step that follows, and with a renewed mind, I can embrace that wherever I am is where I am supposed to be. That all is well regardless of feelings and difficulties that emerge. As I exercise trust, a process is evoked that translates into living in the present moment of consciousness and having the experience of grace, support, love, and knowing that I am changing. I shift into my future self.

The next thing we must examine is conformity vs. transformation. Conformity is the tendency to align our attitudes, beliefs, and behaviors with those around us. It's a powerful force that can take the form of overt social pressure or subtler, unconscious influence. As much as we like to think of ourselves as individuals, the fact is that we're driven to fit in with others and that usually means going with the flow. Conformity is often motivated by our identification with a specific group. To be truly accepted as a member of the group, we must adopt the group norms or the unspoken set of rules that governs their behavior.

When we conform, we outwardly agree with the group consensus, though it may differ from our own personal views. In time, our beliefs and attitudes may begin to shift as we take on the same behaviors and opinions as the rest of our group. We go along to get along, and then we blend in and end up becoming someone that is really beneath us, and we, in turn, can't live our best life. Some people find their definition in the company of other people, and as a result, we never step into true identity. Whenever you are defined from another source other than God, then you rob the world of knowing you. Yielding to the pressures of groups is the epitome of what the text is talking against. He doesn't conform. Don't succumb to the pattern that is set. Don't succumb to the thinking patterns and mindset of other groups that are connected to the system of the world.

The only way to not conform is that I have to come out of agreement with the thoughts from the system that will ultimately lead to hell and destruction. My conformity is connected to what I agree with. Whatever you agree with, you make mental contact with to abide by. If I conform to the world, then I'm making a contract with hell that I will serve your mandate. It's called compliance when you go with the public over your own belief system. Oftentimes when you don't have your own mind or your own views, then you let others dictate who you are and what to think. Oftentimes that can come even from our environment growing up. We are told what to think and what to believe about life. In some cases, about God and its flawed view and God wants to deprogram us and reveal himself to us in ways we would have never known.

Internalization always involves public and private conformity. A person publicly changes their behavior to fit in with the group while also agreeing with them privately. This is the deepest level of conformity where the beliefs of the group become part of the individual's belief system. This means the change in behavior is permanent. We see this in the religious groups that indoctrinate other people into religious beliefs, and then we will completely change our mindset and viewpoints on what we formally knew. People leave God for other beliefs because they have internalized the mindset of other groups. Typically, this change takes place when the people that are influencing us have more knowledge than we do. There are some people who know more about our bible and our God than we do. When you can't match their knowledge with the truth, then at times, it's easy to be swayed because they become believable. That's why we always have to study to show ourselves approved. We have to always be ready to defend our faith amidst people that don't believe like us. Most times, this conformity is because of a personal fear of rejection. That says I don't want to be rejected by this group of people, so I'll do whatever they do so that they don't put me aside. It's the devil's way of keeping us in mental bondage.

He never wants us to step into the definition of who God has made us to be. That's why you can't let other people be the voice of affirmation in your life. You have to know how to affirm yourself and speak over your life what God had declared about you! Conformity also happens when we consult the wrong source of information. You have to be very sure that if you are of the kingdom that you consult kingdom resources for viable information. The other thing we must address is the slave mentality that we have from being tied to the system of the government. That's why we are so stuck on the government, and they dictate what you can do, what you can have, and what you can be. That's slavery!

We need to have our minds free so that we can be what God wants us to be and have what he wants us to have! The government wants to give us their options! God wants to show us that he can show up and work on our behalf if we would let him change our mindset. The children of Israel had this issue with Moses and being free from Egypt. They always wanted to go back to comfortable thinking. They were so comfortable living in slavery that they couldn't think of living free. They rather have a human master rather than a heavenly one. That's the mindset of most people. They can't fathom living in real freedom, so they keep relying on an earthy master; Drugs, alcohol, strip clubs, and all the vices that are connected to the earth. It becomes their master! We conform our lives, and then we march to the beat, rhythm, and pace of the thing that controls us, and not what God is trying to bring us to, and that's real freedom! To truly come out, I have to be changed into a person that I was not previously!

When it comes to transformation, it is to be changed into another form. In that form, we learn things. In a world rapidly changing, each of us is desperately seeking safety. We are being directed to look inward and create a more spiritual life. Illusions are falling away and holding on causes suffering. Changing, we confront broken and fearful parts of ourselves, release the ways in which we limit and control our world, and awaken to the realm of infinite possibility. To release our fear of change, we must trust, whether it is trust in God. We have to be reprogrammed by the Holy Spirit so that we can begin to live our lives with intentionality and purpose.

We have to believe that there is more to life than the physical plane, and we have to mentally develop to live in co-operation with greater intelligence and spiritual truths. We do not know it all, but we, through the transforming power of the Holy Ghost, can be open to new and more evolved ways of being. I accept that there are perspectives larger than my own, benevolent forces that willingly assist me and that I can access divine aspects of my own being. These beliefs are choices we have made that allow a fluidity that invites change. Consequently, where before fear ruled, now new courage to explore and understand emerges at the core of every decision I make. When I am faced with the choice to change, I choose to honor what I know is in alignment with my highest evolution.

Whether this knowing occurs through synchronicity or intuition, whether it shows up as a sick feeling in my stomach, a sense of excitement, an image, or a word in my mind, I trust that what I am receiving is important and worthy of note. I choose to put down the restrictions of linear thinking and allow this knowledge of the Holy Ghost to influence me. I recreate myself out of what I intuit and believe possible, rather than out of my fears. As I do this over and over, I build new muscle. I create a new reality. I step into what real transformation is like because I'm no longer dominated by fear; I'm ruled by my faith!

The final admonition of this text is a change of mind equal to a change of eye vantage. The last part of verse 2 says, so that you may prove what the will of God is, that which is good and acceptable and perfect. Prove is the Greek word dokimazô, meaning to test. With a changed mind, then my perception changes so that I have the spirit of discerning, with God's eye, what his will is for my life. I'm no longer left in the dark about seeing what God has planned for my life once the Holy Spirit is done, giving me a mindset reset. I can see clearer with a better mind. I'm no longer guessing that I have been made by divine design. I have new eyes that I can see that God has a plan for my life and that his plan for me is perfect. Now I can prove and follow the will God has for me. The only way I'm going to gain victory over the world is by a changed mindset!

CHAPTER 10

GOING FROM TRIAL TO TRIUMPH

James 1:2-3 (ESV)

² Count it all joy, my brothers, when you meet trials of various kinds,

³ for you know that the testing of your faith produces steadfastness.

There's an old saying that says," When life hands you lemons, make lemonade." That's always easier to say than to do is what I have discovered because any of us that have gone through life understand that life can throw some things at us that literally has the ability to bring us to our knees. Things that we face in our lives, if we aren't careful, have the proclivity to make us think we are victims. The victim mentality diminishes our ability to see past the present problem. The perception of the victim believes that this is just my lot in life, and things won't get any better than where I am. The issue with that perception is that it hinders our ability to step into the realm of victory.

I think we need to resolve that being a victor is a decision. We can't dictate the situations that come up in our lives, but we do have the power to decide that we are going to be overcomers. We have to decide that whatever state we find ourselves in, we are going to be content because we know that we can do all things through Christ that gives us strength. I have to make a decision that even when I am faced with a victim like situation, that I am going to decide to be a victor no matter what.

We can see this made clear in this James passage. What James is saying to us here is that we can have the ability to move from the victim to the victor and experience a life of winning if we deal with our perception. Whether we are being tested internally or externally, we have to decide the outcome. If I decide to stay in the mindset of a victim, then I'll never move to the next level in God. If I decide to move to the realm of victory, then what I gain as a byproduct is spiritual maturity.

What that suggests is that outlook determines the outcome. In the area of perception, how I see what I see determines how it will end up in my life. The reason being is that attitude follows action. My attitude in the process will determine what I do. If I trust God, then my action will be reflective of that attitude. If I trust my flesh and my own ability over God, then my action will be reflective of that. The issue is the outcome. If I trust God, then it will work in my favor. If I rely on my flesh, then I'll always be attempting but never arriving at the place God has designed. The main aim of God is to lead us as his people into maturation. What this passage tells us is that we have to expect trials.

That's what James doesn't say if you fall into divers' temptations, but rather he says when you fall into divers' temptations. That's a definite fact that you and I will encounter trials. I think people get shell shocked when things come on us because we didn't expect it. We have been bamboozled into believing that just because we are saved and know God that we won't encounter life. James prepares us because he says to us that life will happen to the best of us. In John 16:33, Jesus warns us that in this life, you will have tribulation. God's people will have to go through some things. We are not meant to be spoiled or sheltered people. We are models and templates. That means that oftentimes we have to go through things in the face of others so that God can show himself mighty and strong in our lives to draw others to him.

Notice that James says, count. Another translation says consider. It's a Greek word hēgeomai that means to evaluate or to think. It's actually a financial term that suggests before you make a big move, you have to evaluate it. Think about it. Here is where the perception comes into play. When we don't see or perceive correctly, then it taints the action and calls the outcome into question. When we face the trials of life, we must evaluate them in the light of what God is doing for us. That becomes the critical question. God, what are you trying to develop in me? When we have the right perception, then we can understand that what looks like disaster is really development. Oftentimes they look the same situationally, but when you know that God is at work in your life, then it becomes the game-changer.

I then can see that the thing that I'm in was never meant to kill me, but it was ultimately meant to grow me. You can't grow unless there is pressure. Something in you has to die in order for there to be growth. For many of us, God is allowing situations to come into our lives to change us. The greatest change takes place under immense pressure when you consider it correctly. That's why for some people, they can have real joy in the midst of pressure because they see it right. People will think you have lost your mind because you're praising God as you endure a hard season. People think that because of what you are facing that you should pull your hair out. What they don't understand is that you know something. What do you know? I know Romans 8:28 is still relevant. We know that God causes all things to work together for good to those who love the Lord and to those who are called according to his purpose.

When we see it right, then it changes our outlook. No longer are we concerned with the devil being on assignment. We start focusing our attention on whatever God is developing inside of us. Our values determine our evaluations. If we value comfort more than character, then trials will upset us. If we value the material and physical more than the spiritual, we will not be able to "count it all joy." If we live only for the present and forget the future, then trials will make us bitter, not better. James says consider, count, think it all joy. Now when we bring up the issue of joy, then we will note that joy is not predicated on the situation.

Anytime we address the issue of joy, we will note that real joy is based on the facts of what I know about God. If we know that God is working through our situations to bring us to a better place of maturity, then we can have joy. We have joy because we know that this is just a process. The process is designed to grow me through it. So, when trials come, immediately give thanks to the Lord, and adopt a joyful attitude. Do not pretend; do not try self-hypnosis; simply look at trials through the eyes of faith. Outlook determines outcome; to *end* with joy, *begin* with joy.

Finally, James says that the testing or the proving of your faith works patience. Whenever God tests, he is testing to increase. God always tests us to bring out the *best;* Satan tempts us to bring out the worst. The testing of our faith proves that we are truly born again. Here is what right perception will do. It will reveal to us that what looks like it's working against us is really working for us. Through the trial, we are gaining approval. God is approving you through the hardship that we face. God's approval of our faith is precious because it assures us that our faith is genuine.

I don't care what you are going through. I don't care how bad things seem to be at the present moment. We have to know that God is working in it, and he is trying to train your eyes to see it right so that you can get the desired outcome of heaven concerning you and me. My final admonition is to go through it. You always win in the end! God is shifting us from trial to triumph!

Made in the USA
Monee, IL
02 June 2021

70009418R00049